William Dwight Whitney

by

Thomas D. Seymour

William Dwight Whitney
by Thomas D. Seymour

ISBN: 978-93-69072-67-5

Published by

DOUBLE 9 BOOKS

2/13-B, Ansari Road
Daryaganj, New Delhi – 110002
info@double9books.com
www.double9books.com
Tel. 011-40042856

ABOUT THE AUTHOR

Thomas Day Seymour was an American classical scholar, born on April 1, 1848, in Hudson, Ohio. He is best known for his career as a Professor of Greek at Yale University, where he dedicated much of his scholarly work to the study of ancient Greek literature, particularly the works of Homer. Seymour was regarded as one of the leading classical scholars of his time and made significant contributions to the academic study of Homeric texts. His expertise in Greek language and literature, along with his detailed analyses of Homer's epics, helped shape the field of classical studies in the United States. Throughout his career, Seymour published numerous works on Greek literature, and his scholarly rigor earned him a respected place among the intellectual elite. Seymour's influence extended beyond his academic work as he also mentored many students who went on to have distinguished careers themselves. He passed away on December 31, 1907, at the age of 59, in New Haven, Connecticut. Seymour's legacy lives on through his contributions to classical scholarship and his impact on the study of ancient Greek texts. He was the father of Charles Seymour and grandfather to Charles Seymour, Jr.

CONTENTS

WILLIAM DWIGHT WHITNEY[1]

Northampton, Massachusetts, half a century ago, was one of the best examples of a typical New England town—among stately hills, on the banks of the Connecticut River, with broad streets well shaded by great spreading elms, with large homesteads still occupied by the descendants of early settlers, with people of much culture and refinement who were given to "plain living and high thinking." It was the town of Edwards, of Dwight, of Hawley, of Stoddard, of Strong, and of many another worthy. It was the seat of the once famous Round Hill Academy. There, on February 9, 1827, William Dwight Whitney was born,—the second surviving son and fourth child of Josiah Dwight Whitney and Sarah Williston Whitney. His mother was a daughter of the Rev. Payson Williston (Yale, 1783), of Easthampton, and sister of the Hon. Samuel Williston, who founded Williston Seminary. His father was born in Westfield, Mass.,—the oldest son of Abel Whitney, who was graduated at Harvard in 1783.

No company of brothers and sisters of any American family has been so remarkable for scholarly attainments and achievements as that family in Northampton: Josiah D. Whitney, Jr. (Yale, 1839), Professor of Geology at Harvard; William D. Whitney, of Yale; James L. Whitney (Yale, 1856), of the Boston Public Library; Henry M. Whitney (Yale, 1864), Professor of English Literature at Beloit College; Miss Maria Whitney, the first incumbent of the chair of Modern Languages in Smith College.

William D. Whitney was fitted for college in his native town, and entered the Sophomore class of Williams College in 1842, at the age of fifteen. Tradition says that the studies of the college course were easy to him, and that he spent most of his time in wandering over the fields, studying geology and the habits of birds and of plants, although he maintained the first rank for scholarship in his class. On his graduation he pronounced the valedictory oration, on 'Literary Biography.'

After graduation—at eighteen, the age when most now enter college—Mr. Whitney remained for three years in uncertainty with regard to his life-work, meanwhile busy as teller in his father's bank. He did not take an active part in the social life of the young people of Northampton, but employed himself in his own pursuits. His leisure time was given largely to the collection of birds and plants; a large and beautiful case of birds stuffed by him at this period is in the Peabody Museum at New Haven. His tastes for natural science were marked, and he was more than an amateur in that field. He spent the summer of 1849 in the United States Survey of the Lake Superior region, conducted by his eminent brother, Josiah D. Whitney—having "under his charge the botany, the ornithology, and the accounts." In the summer of 1873, also, he was invited to take part in the Hayden exploring expedition in Colorado. The Report of the Survey says that he "rendered most valuable assistance ... in geographical work." His account of this expedition of 1873 was published in the New York *Tribune*, and afterwards was translated into French for a popular publication of that country, as giving a clear view of the work of such scientific parties. He had a brief article in the *American Journal of Science* for the same year on the U. S. Geological Survey of the Territories. He gave several months of his time just before leaving home for his last visit to Europe, to helping Professor J. D. Whitney put through the press the latter's work on 'The Metallic Wealth of the United States.'

His scientific experience stood him in good stead in more than one instance of philological research and discussion. He was not tempted to infer from linguistic data the order of succession of trees in forests, nor astronomical facts. He was a member for several years of the American Association for the Advancement of Science. One of his most important publications was the annotated translation of a Hindu treatise on astronomy—the Sūrya-Siddhānta, 1860—and one of the longest essays in his 'Oriental and Linguistic Studies' treats of the same subject.

In 1848, largely under the influence and with the encouragement of his father's pastor, the Rev. George E. Day (for a quarter of a century after 1866 Professor of Hebrew at Yale, and at present Dean of the Yale Divinity School), Mr. Whitney directed his attention to the study of Sanskrit, for which he found books in the library of his elder brother, who had recently returned from Europe. A really good mind can find pleasure and success in any one of several different fields of research. Not often, however, do we find such marked examples of men of real talent manifesting distinct tastes and power in widely different departments of learning as in the case of these two brothers. Mr. J. D. Whitney went to Germany primarily in order to prepare himself for mineralogical and geological work, but became interested in the study of languages and attended (with but two fellow-listeners) a course of lectures on Sanskrit at Berlin. He himself says that he might have taken up philology in earnest, abandoning natural science altogether, if immediately after his return to his home he had not received an appointment to engage in a geological survey of a new and interesting region under United States authority. His philological studies have borne fruit in his 'Names and Places—Studies in Geographical and Topographical Nomenclature,' published in 1888, and in the more than four thousand definitions he furnished to the Century Dictionary. Mr. W. D. Whitney certainly had great ability in the study of natural science. Doubtless the accident of his finding various linguistic books ready to hand, at the time when his mental powers were most actively developing, had much to do with his turning in the direction of philology. During the summer which he spent with his brother on Lake Superior he had a Sanskrit grammar with him, which he studied at odd moments when not engaged in collecting plants or computing barometrical observations. Yale College has had another marked example of a scholar with equal ability and tastes for widely diverse studies, in Professor James Hadley, whose first published work was in the department of mathematics, and of whom a high authority said that the best mathematician in the country was spoiled when Mr. Hadley devoted himself to Greek!

Mr. Whitney's practical banker father was not fully satisfied with his plan of giving himself to Oriental studies, and asked his pastor whether a man could support himself in life by studying and teaching Sanskrit. Dr. Day made the very wise answer that if a man had any exact and thorough knowledge, he was likely to be able to use it. As a Massachusetts man, the father turned naturally to Harvard as the proper place for his son's pursuit of advanced studies, but his pastor called his attention to the newly established department of Philosophy and the Arts at New Haven as the only definite arrangement yet made in this country for university work, and especially to the unique equipment of the special department of Oriental languages.

Before going to New Haven to study, Mr. Whitney prepared and published in the *Bibliotheca Sacra* an article (translated and abridged from von Bohlen) on the 'Grammatical Structure of the Sanskrit'; and in the same periodical, in the following year, he published a 'Comparison of the Greek and Latin Verbs.'

In the autumn of 1849, too late for his name to appear in the catalogue of that year, Mr. Whitney came to Yale and studied through the remainder of the college year under Professor Salisbury. His associate in study was Professor James Hadley (six years older than himself, but only three years older in college age), who had been appointed assistant professor of Greek in 1848. The relations of the two continued most intimate and mutually stimulating until the death of Professor Hadley in 1872. Mr. Whitney edited a volume of Professor Hadley's Essays, in 1873, and wrote a brief but highly appreciative sketch of his friend for the large work entitled 'Yale College,' published in 1879.

Professor Salisbury was graduated at Yale in 1832. During more than three years' residence abroad, 1836-39, he studied with De Sacy and Garcin de Tassy in Paris and with Bopp in Berlin. In 1841 he was invited to a professorship of the Arabic and Sanskrit languages in Yale College, without the expectation of pecuniary compensation. This was only nine years after the foundation of the Sanskrit professorship (of H. H. Wilson) at Oxford, and twelve years after Lassen was made Professor Extraordinarius at Bonn. He returned to Europe in 1842 for a year, and read *privatissime* Arabic with Freytag and Sanskrit with Lassen, at Bonn. In 1846 he was made the Corresponding Secretary of the American Oriental Society, and (to use Mr. Whitney's words) "for some ten years Professor Salisbury was virtually the Society, doing its work and paying its bills. He gave it standing and credit in the world of scholars, as an organization that could originate and make public valuable material; after such a start, it was sure of respectful attention to whatever it might do." The Society had published nothing before he took charge of this office. Professor Salisbury also secured valuable Arabic and Sanskrit manuscripts and books from De Sacy's library and elsewhere in Europe; and Professor FitzEdward Hall, then at Benares, procured for him many expensive and important Sanskrit publications from India. His services and generosity in procuring fonts of Oriental type, and his wisdom in bringing the Oriental Society into close connection with the studies of foreign missionaries, should not be forgotten. He was the only trained Orientalist in this country, until Mr. Whitney's return in 1853, and had an admirably equipped library. In the Yale catalogue of 1841-42, Professor Salisbury's name appears for the first time in the list of the faculty as Professor of the Arabic and Sanskrit Languages and Literature. In the catalogue of 1843-44, announcement is made that "the Professor of Arabic and Sanskrit will give instruction on Tuesdays and Wednesdays in Arabic grammar with the interpretation of the Korân and the Mo'allakas, and on Fridays and Saturdays in Sanskrit grammar with the interpretation of the laws of Manu." In the following year we are told that "the Professor of Arabic and Sanskrit proposes to commence this year, in the ensuing summer, a free course of lectures on the Sacred Code of the Hindus, the Manava Dharma Sastra." In 1845 for the first time appears a modestly-placed paragraph, saying "Instruction is also given by the Professors to Resident Graduates, provided a sufficient number present themselves to form a class." This was followed by the offer of a "course of lectures on the literary history and doctrines of the Kurân," or instruction in the elements of Sanskrit. In 1847 appeared the formal announcement of the opening of the Department of Philosophy and the Arts, with definite arrangements for advanced work. The philological courses were by President Woolsey (Thucydides or Pindar), Professor Kingsley ("in such Latin author as may be agreed upon"), Professor Gibbs ("lectures on some points of general Philology"), and Professor Salisbury (Arabic Grammar, and "some of the relations of the Arabic to other of the Shemitish dialects").

Marvellous stories are told in student-tradition of the rapid progress made by Mr. Whitney and Mr. Hadley—that they learned all the paradigms of Bopp's grammar in two lessons, etc. The basis of the stories is partly the fact that both already read simple Sanskrit with ease, but it is certain that few teachers ever had such a class. They were Professor Salisbury's first and last pupils in Sanskrit, but he might well feel proud of the record. He himself says of them that "their quickness of perception and unerring exactness of acquisition soon made it evident that the teacher and the taught must change places."

In 1850 Mr. Whitney went to Germany and spent three winter semesters in studying with Weber, Bopp, and Lepsius in Berlin, and two summer semesters at work with Roth in Tübingen. At the suggestion of Roth he undertook with this master the publication of the Atharva-Veda, and copied and collated the Berlin MSS of this work. In 1852 he sent to the American Oriental Society a paper, read at their October meeting of that year, on 'The main results of the later Vedic researches in Germany.' A letter from Weber, dated at Berlin, Dec. 28, 1852, is interesting in this connection on several accounts. He writes: "I hope ere long Sanskrit studies will flourish in America more than in England, where with the only exception of the venerable and not-to-be-praised-enough Professor Wilson nobody seems to care for them so much as to devote his life to them. The East India Company certainly does all that is in its power to help the publication of the Vedic texts, but it does not find English hands to achieve it.... It is certainly very discouraging to see that Professor Wilson during all the time since he got his professorship in Oxford, has not succeeded in bringing up even one Sanskrit scholar who might claim to be regarded as one who has done at least some little service to our Sanskrit philology.... I have to congratulate you most heartily on your countryman Mr. Whitney, who is now intensely engaged in the preparations for an edition of the Atharva Samhitā in union with Professor Roth of Tübingen. The next number of the *Indische Studien*, too, which is now in press, contains from him tables showing the natural relation of the four now known Samhitās of the Veda,—an attempt in which he was greatly indebted to Professor Roth's communications, but which still remains also a very favorable specimen of his own assiduity and correctness."

The following letters need little explanation. We note with interest how soon the first followed the receipt of Weber's letter which has just been quoted. The spirit which prompted the offer of the first letter is certainly unusual in its generosity—not only surrendering a professorial chair, but also providing for its endowment. The modesty and delicacy of the reply seem as extraordinary at the present day, and were perhaps as rare forty years ago.

Under date of February 19, 1853, Professor Salisbury wrote to Mr. Whitney: "... I have observed your course of study and the rapidity of your acquisitions since you have been abroad with much interest and have seen in this, together with what I have known otherwise of your tastes and talents, a way opening for relief to myself which I have long desired. The prospect has been the more pleasing to me inasmuch as I have also seen that I might be able through you to bring new honor to my 'alma mater.'... It is also much at heart with me to secure ... assistance to myself in editing and endeavouring in every way to improve the Journal of the Oriental Society." Professor Salisbury proposed that Mr. Whitney should be made "Professor of the Sanskrit and its relations to the kindred languages, and of Sanskrit literature, in the Department of Philosophy and the Arts in Yale College," his term of service to begin Aug. 8, 1853;—it being understood that Mr. Whitney would include in his instructions the teaching of modern languages to undergraduates, and should receive the fees which were then paid for such teaching. It was understood, further, that Mr. Whitney would co-operate with Professor Salisbury in editing the Journal of the Oriental Society. Professor Salisbury undertook to create a fund which with the fees for modern-language instruction might furnish nearly the ordinary salary of a Yale professor at that time.

Mr. Whitney replied from Paris, on April 4, 1853. Professor Salisbury's letter had reached him at Berlin at a time when he was engaged in closing his work there, and "had hardly an hour for quiet thought upon any subject." He expressed his gratitude for the kind feeling toward him "which has had a share in the dictating of the proposal," and continued: "Nor can I well say how much I am struck by the true and self-forgetting zeal for the progress of Oriental studies, of which this, like all your previous movements, affords an evidence. But ... I am compelled to ask myself whether ... I can hope to render any such service to Science as would be an adequate return for the kindness you exhibit toward me; whether, finally, it would not be in me an act of unpardonable presumption to take upon my shoulders an office which you are desirous of throwing off.... I need not say how high and honorable a post I regard that of a teacher at Yale to be, how many and extreme attractions, both in a personal and in a scientific point of view, the prospect of such a situation would have for me.... So far as my own interests are concerned, I could find nothing in the terms which you propose or the duties which you suggest to which to raise a moment's objection.... All that I could bring up against the arrangement would be that the advantage is too entirely upon my side." He desired further time for reflection and consultation with his friends, and thought the postponement of a decision less objectionable because he did not expect to be able to finish his work in Europe and return before the last of August, and then, after a three years' absence from home, desired to spend some time with his friends. His eyes, too, had been giving him "during the winter ground for some apprehension," and "would doubtless be best consulted for by a period of rest and inaction."

In Paris he was "at work on a MS of the Atharva which belongs to the Imperial Library." "Probably it will cost me about six weeks' labor.... Then will follow two or three months of similar labor in London and Oxford.... During the whole winter I was compelled to neglect all other studies; that, however, chiefly owing to the condition of my eyes, which robbed me of about half my time. Persian and Arabic had to be laid aside altogether, and what of time and strength I had to spare from the Sanskrit, I devoted to the Egyptian and Coptic. I cannot well express to you the interest which this latter branch of study has awakened in me, and the strong desire I have felt to penetrate further into it than the mere surface exploration which could be made in the odd moments of a single winter. I would not, however, sell for a very large sum the little insight into this wonderful subject which I have already obtained, and it will be my highest pleasure to attempt to draw it somewhat more into the circle of our Oriental inquiries than has been generally the case hitherto.... There is nothing new of particular interest, so far as I know, to communicate to you from the Sanskrit world on this side of the water. The main interest attaches to the Lexicon which is going to be really a great work, and to push forward the whole study of that language a long way with one thrust. A slow thrust, unfortunately, it will have to be; Prof. Roth estimates ten years as needed for its perfection. [It was completed in 1875.] I am going to contribute my small mite also toward it, by furnishing to Prof. Roth the vocabulary complete of the Atharva. The latter, as you perhaps know, has now the sole redaction of the Vedic material, Aufrecht having left Germany. The next number of Weber's Zeitschrift will be out now very soon, and will contain a contribution from me, a Vedic concordance."

Mr. Whitney reached home earlier than he had expected—about Aug. 8, 1853—and on Aug. 15 he wrote: "Although not less distrustful than before of my ability to discharge to your satisfaction and my own the duties of the post to which you would assign me, I should be disposed to accept gratefully your proposals, and do my best at least to accomplish that which such an acceptance demands of me." But Mr. Whitney desired a modification of the plan. "I have no such knowledge of French as would in any manner justify me in making pretensions to ability to teach it." His estimate of his knowledge of modern languages was lower than that of his friends. Not until 1856 did he accept the title of "Instructor in German." A year later, after he had taken nine months of travel and study in southern Europe, the college catalogue calls him "Professor of Sanskrit, and Instructor in modern languages."

The importance to American scholarship of the offer of this chair to Professor Whitney may be better appreciated if we remember that his predecessor still lives, and that no other chair of Sanskrit was established in this country for about a quarter of a century.

At a special meeting of the Corporation of Yale College, on May 10, 1854, the "Professorship of the Sanskrit and its relations to kindred languages, and Sanskrit Literature" was established, and Mr. Whitney was elected to hold it. The founder's desire for the range of the department was indicated distinctly, but the shorter name of the professorship, "Professor of Sanskrit," was used in the college catalogues until 1869, when the words "and Comparative Philology" were added, without indicating any change in the direction of the incumbent's studies or in the plan of the university.

In 1854 the announcement of philological courses in the Department of Philosophy and the Arts covered Professor Gibbs's lectures on general Philology, Professor Thacher's course of two hours a week in Lucretius and in Latin Composition, Professor Hadley's course of two hours a week in Pindar or Theocritus, and contained the following statement: "Professor Whitney will give instruction in Sanskrit from Bopp's Grammar and Nalus, or such other text-books as may be agreed upon, and in the rudiments of the Ancient and Modern Persian, and of the Egyptian languages." The last clause here reminds the reader of the enthusiasm for the Egyptian and Coptic expressed in the letter of April 4, 1853; and of the fact that Mr. Whitney's first 'bibliographical notice' in the Journal of the Oriental Society discussed Lepsius's work on the 'First order of Egyptian deities,' but we read little more of these studies, except a paper on Lepsius's Nubian Grammar in the second volume of this Journal. In 1858 Professor Whitney's announcement read: "Professor Whitney will instruct in the Sanskrit language, and in the History, Antiquities, and Literature of India and other Oriental countries; also in the comparative philology of the Indo-European languages, and the general principles of linguistic study. He will also give instruction to such as may desire it in the modern European languages."

The appointment of Professor Whitney in 1854 was for five years, with a pledge of reappointment "for life," five years later, if he desired it. In 1859 this reappointment was made—the founder of the chair stipulating that Professor Whitney should be free to retire from the professorship at any time. Mr. Whitney wrote, on July 15, 1859: "My present situation in New Haven is so pleasant to me on so many accounts, and holds out such prospects of honorable and useful employment in the time to come, that I should exceedingly regret being compelled to go elsewhere. Nor, although it would be in many respects more agreeable to me to be able to devote my *whole* time to my own peculiar studies, do I see reason seriously to regret the division of my labors between the ancient and the modern languages. It is both useful and pleasant to have to do more directly with the young men in college, and there is also the chance of influencing one and another of them to devote his attention to higher philological study."

During and after the Civil War, the ordinary expenses of life increased, and Mr. Whitney's family was growing. The income which had sufficed for the young and unmarried professor in 1854 had become entirely insufficient for his needs, with six children, in 1870. For his pecuniary relief he assumed additional duties of instruction in modern languages, in connection with the Sheffield Scientific School. His teaching of modern languages in the academic department had ceased with the entrance upon his duties of Professor Coe, in 1867. The burden of instructing large classes of undergraduates in the very rudiments of French and German (each Academic student then having only thirty or forty lessons in each subject) became more and more irksome.

In September, 1869, Mr. Whitney received an urgent call to Harvard, very soon after President Eliot's election to the headship of that university, with the assurance that he should have "salary enough to constitute a tolerable support," and should not have to teach in any other than his own proper department. He wrote to a friend: "It is the most tempting offer that could, so far as I know, be made me; for on the one hand I have greatly grudged the time which I have had to steal from Oriental and linguistic studies for German and French; and, on the other hand, what I have received for my services to the College has not for a good while paid more than about half my expenses.... Such a state of things has been, of course, worrying enough, nor have I seen any definite prospect of a change. But I am greatly attached to the College here, and to the Scientific School, and to relatives and friends in New Haven, and have no hope that ... I should become so wonted and so comfortable anywhere else."

Professor Whitney's colleagues saw how fatal his departure would be to the advanced philological work at Yale. No definite provision had then been made for graduate instruction in Greek, Latin, and Modern Languages, and although Professors Hadley, Thacher, Packard, and Coe were laboring to build up this department, their efforts received only the slightest pecuniary compensation; they were expected to do full work in the undergraduate department; Mr. Whitney was the only "University professor," not only at Yale, but in the whole country. One who is everywhere recognized as a leader in education then wrote: "I am confident that there is no one whose intellectual influence over the younger officers of the college is so great as Mr. Whitney's.... I have greatly admired his influence in promoting fidelity, truth, justice, and industry among the students, as well as his skill in promoting their intellectual character." Another of his colleagues wrote: "I have never known the college men so moved. The danger of losing so eminent a man as Mr. Whitney seemed almost appalling, and I think if no other means of retaining him could be devised, the professors themselves would each cut off a slice from his meagre salary to make up the amount necessary to retain him. The question seems to rise above personal considerations and to come very near to the vital interests of the university."

Professor Salisbury, whose insight and generosity had brought Mr. Whitney to Yale, was nearly concerned by the call to Cambridge, and after less than a week's delay provided the sum needed for the full foundation of Mr. Whitney's chair on the modern scale of salaries, which had changed greatly since 1854, and Mr. Whitney decided to remain in New Haven. At this time the arrangement was made that Mr. Whitney should give regular instruction in linguistics to the undergraduate classes of the college, and this course, at first given in the form of lectures, as part of the required work, was amplified and continued as an 'elective' until 1886. Mr. Whitney still continued to teach in the Scientific School for an hour a day, saying that in no other way could he add so easily a convenient thousand dollars a year to his income as by teaching from eight to nine o'clock each morning; he required no preparation for the exercise, it did not interfere with the work of his day, and he liked to be brought into contact with the young men.

The invitation to Harvard and the decision to remain at Yale had attracted considerable attention and had given rise to many plans for advanced philological instruction at New Haven. Mr. Whitney's release from drudgery with undergraduates enabled him also to enrich his Sanskrit and linguistic courses. In the catalogue of 1870-71 we read: "In Philology, a somewhat regular course of higher study, extending through two years, and leading to the degree of Doctor of Philosophy, is offered. The leading studies of the first year will be The general principles of linguistic science, under Professor Whitney; the Sanskrit language, under Professor Whitney; the older Germanic languages, especially Gothic and Anglo-Saxon, under Professor Hadley and Mr. Lounsbury; along with higher instruction in the classical and the modern languages, according to the special requirements of each student, under Professors Thacher, Packard, and Coe, and Messrs. Van Name and Lounsbury, and others. The leading studies of the second year will be The comparative philology of the Indo-European languages ... under Professor Whitney; the history of the English language, under Professor Hadley; along with other special branches, as during the first year." The reward for the new enterprise of a formal graduate school of philology came almost immediately in the form of an unusual class of students, nearly all of whom were destined to secure honorable distinction in their chosen work. In the list of those who received the degree of Ph.D. in 1873 appear the names of Lanman of Harvard, Learned of the Japanese Doshisha, Luquiens of Yale, Manatt of Brown, Otis of the Institute of Technology, and Perrin of Yale. Truly an unusual group! Only the year before, Professor Easton of the University of Pennsylvania and Professor Beckwith of Trinity College, and the year following Professor Edgren of the University of Gothenburg, received the same degree, while soon after them President Harper of Chicago, Professor H. P. Wright of Yale, Professor Sherman of Nebraska, Professor Peters of the University of Pennsylvania, and Professor Tarbell of the University of Chicago completed the graduate course under Mr. Whitney. The service which the Semitic scholar, Professor George E. Day, had done for Indo-European philology by turning Professor Whitney's mind to its attractions, was in a way repaid by the latter when he pointed out to William Rainey Harper the great opportunity open to workers in the Semitic field; as a graduate student at Yale, Dr. Harper gave himself to work in the field of the Indo-European languages, but his recollection of his master's words has had a wide influence on Semitic studies in America. Professor Whitney was justly proud of his pupils, and was always interested in their work. His classes in Sanskrit were not large absolutely, but frequently he could say that more were studying this language with him than with any other university professor in the world.

Professor Whitney's connection with the Sheffield Scientific School was close. He organized its department of modern languages, and was a member of its 'Governing Board' from the time of the organization of that body in 1872. One who has occasion to know better than all others says that he was "a tower of strength" to the School—not only by his instructions and by inspiring the students with the spirit of true scholarship, but by his intelligent appreciation of the aims of the School and his wise judgment as to the means to be used in order to attain them. His personal liking for natural science, and training in its methods, added the warmest sympathy to his work in connection with this department of the University.

In the very first communication made to Mr. Whitney with regard to his work at Yale, attention was called to the opportunity for usefulness in connection with the American Oriental Society, of which he was elected a member in 1850. In 1854 his name appears in the list of the publication committee of that Society. In 1855 he was made librarian, and held that office until 1873. This latter post was no sinecure. In the winter of 1853-54, on going to visit the library (then kept in Boston), he "found it a pile of books on the floor in the corner of an upstairs room in the Athenaeum, apparently just as it had been brought in and dumped down from an earlier place of keeping." In the summer of 1855 the books were removed to New Haven. The task of "arranging, labelling, entering in the book of donations, and preparing cards" involved "a very considerable and tedious amount of work." In 1857, on Professor Salisbury's going abroad and resigning the office, Professor Whitney was elected Corresponding Secretary, and continued in this position until 1884, when he was elected President of the Society. His resignation of this latter office was not accepted until 1890, when for nearly four years the condition of his health had obliged him to absent himself from its meetings. He could well say that "no small part of his work had been done in the service of the Society"; from 1857 to 1885, "just a half of the contents of its Journal is from his pen." His care of the publications of others, also, was specially difficult, in view of the peculiar danger of typographical errors and the wide field covered by the papers; no ordinary proof-reader could render much assistance. And not infrequently articles by those who were unaccustomed to scientific composition needed thorough revision. On his positively declining to be a candidate for re-election as President, the Society adopted the following minute: "The American Oriental Society— regretfully accepting his declination—desires to record its deep sense of indebtedness to its retiring President, Professor William Dwight Whitney, of New Haven. For twenty-seven years he has served as Corresponding Secretary of the Society; for eighteen, as its Librarian; and for six, as its President. We gratefully acknowledge the obligation under which he has laid us by his diligent attendance at the meetings, by his unstinted giving of time and of labor in editing the publications and maintaining their high scientific character, by the quality and amount of his own contributions to the *Journal*—more than half of volumes VI-XII coming from his pen—and above all by the inspiration of his example."

The American Philological Association might have been a natural off-shoot from the Oriental Society. The latter has had a 'classical-section' since 1849, of which Professor Hadley was long at the head, of which Professor Goodwin has been the leader for nearly a quarter of a century; and classical papers had been presented by Professor Hadley, as that 'On the theory of

Greek accent,' and by Professor Lane, as that 'On the date of the Amphitruo of Plautus.' Many of the early members of the Philological Association were also members of the Oriental Society. Mr. Whitney presided over the Philological Association at its first meeting in Poughkeepsie in 1869, and at the Rochester meeting in 1870, as retiring President, he delivered an address in which he sketched with great wisdom the Association's action and work. "The association is to be just what its members shall make it, and will not bear much managing or mastering. It must discuss the subjects which are interesting American philologists, and with such wisdom and knowledge as these have at command.... In every such free and democratic body things are brought forward into public which might better have been kept back.... The classics, of course, will occupy the leading place; that department will be most strongly represented, and will least need fostering, while it will call for most careful criticism. The philology of the American aboriginal languages, on the other hand, demands, as it has already begun to receive, the most hearty encouragement.... Educational subjects also are closely bound up with philology, and will necessarily receive great attention; yet there should be a limit here; our special task is to advance the interests of philology only, confident that education will reap its share of the benefit." Mr. Whitney's services to the Association, and faithful attendance upon its meetings, may be estimated from the fact that the first sixteen volumes of the Transactions contain fourteen papers by him printed in full, while occasionally he presented communications which he did not care to print. At its meeting in Williamstown in July last, the Association adopted the following minute: "The American Philological Association, at its first meeting after the death of Professor William D. Whitney, bears grateful testimony to the value of the services which he rendered for the furtherance of philological learning, and especially in connection with this Association. Fitly chosen to be its first President, and retained for a quarter of a century upon its Executive Committee, he never failed to take an active part in its work, and in many ways he advanced its interests and encouraged and assisted the studies to which its members are devoted. The record of his life-work may be left for more full recital at another time; but the Association takes this opportunity of testifying to its sense of obligation to Professor Whitney's manifold and successful labors, and of the great loss which his death has brought to its members and to philological students throughout the world."

Both the classical and the oriental philologists of the country have noted Mr. Whitney's constancy in attendance on their gatherings. In November, 1875, he apologized to the Oriental Society for his absence from the May meeting (caused by his visit to Europe in the interest of the edition of the Atharva-Veda), and added that it was his second absence in twenty-one years from a meeting of the Society! His devoted fidelity to the little Classical and Philological Society at Yale was just as marked. A quarter of a century ago, he with Professor Hadley and Professor Packard made that small gathering a deep source of inspiration. Many, if not most, of his learned papers were presented for discussion there. After the death of the lamented Professor Hadley, which gave a sudden check to the development of Yale's advanced courses in philology, Mr. Whitney was the mainstay of the Society, and his regular attendance and patient attention roused to best effort each who took part. Perhaps I ought to confess also that some of the younger instructors and graduate students shrank from presenting papers which might be compared with the finished scholar's elaborate productions. At these meetings his patience must have been sorely tried; much that was presented can have had but little interest for him; but his courtesy was unfailing. He gave without stint of his precious time to any undertaking which he believed to be doing, on the whole, useful philological work.

The first great work of Mr. Whitney's scholarship was the publication of the Atharva-Veda-Sanhitā, undertaken in 1852 with Professor Roth. The first volume of 458 pages, royal octavo, was published in 1855-56. In connection with this, he prepared and published in Weber's *Indische Studien* (vol. IV, pp. 9-64) in 1857 an 'Alphabetisches Verzeichniss der Versanfänge der Atharva-Samhitā'; in the *Journal* of the American Oriental Society in 1862 (vol. VII, pp. 333-616) the 'Atharva-Veda-Prātiçākhya,' with text, translation and notes; in the same *Journal* in 1881 (vol. XII, pp. 1-383) an 'Index Verborum' to the published text of the Atharva-Veda. He made to the A.O.S. in April, 1892, an 'Announcement' as to a second volume of the Roth-Whitney edition of the Atharva-Veda. "The bulk of the work" of preparing notes, indexes, etc., "was to have fallen to Professor Roth, not only because the bulk of the work on the first volume had fallen to me [i. e. Professor Whitney], but also because his superior learning and ability pointed him out as the one to undertake it." But Roth's "absorption in the great labor of the Petersburg lexicon for a long series of years had kept his hands from the Atharva-Veda." Mr. Whitney said that he had never lost from view the completion of the plan of publication as originally formed. "In 1875 I spent the summer in Germany chiefly engaged in further collating at Munich and at Tübingen the additional manuscript material which had come to Europe since our text was printed; and I should probably have soon taken up the work seriously, save for having been engaged while in Germany to prepare a Sanskrit grammar, which fully occupied the leisure of several following years. At last in 1885-86, I had fairly started upon the execution of the plan when failure of health reduced my working capacity to a minimum, and rendered ultimate success very questionable. The task, however, has never been laid wholly aside, and it is now so far advanced that barring further loss of power, I may hope to finish it in a couple of years or so. The plan includes critical readings upon the text"; the readings of the Pāippalāda version; the data of the Anukramaṇī respecting authorship, divinity, and meter of each verse; references to the ancillary literature; extracts from the printed commentary; and, finally, a simple literal translation. "An introduction and indexes will give such further material as appears to be called for." Of this work the last revision is only partially made; a few months' more labor would have completed it; Professor Lanman, of Harvard, has undertaken to finish the revision and to conduct the volume through the press. Thus Professor Whitney's work closes as it began—with the Atharva-Veda.

Perhaps Mr. Whitney's most important service to Sanskrit philology was the preparation of his 'Sanskrit Grammar, including both the classical language, and the older dialects, of Veda and Brahmana,' 486 pp., octavo. This was published in Leipzig in 1879, in the same year with a German translation. He undertook this work in 1875, and in 1878 went to Germany with his family and spent fifteen months in writing out the grammar and preparing it for the press. He aimed "to make a presentation of the facts of the language primarily as they show themselves in use in the literature, and only secondarily as they are laid down by the native grammarians"; "to include also in the presentation the forms and constructions of the older language, as exhibited in the Veda and Brāhmaṇa"; "to treat the language throughout as an accented one"; "to cast all statements, classifications, and so on, into a form consistent with the teachings of linguistic science." "While the treatment of the facts of the language has thus been made a historical one, within the limits of the language itself, I have not ventured to make it comparative, by bringing in the analogous forms and processes of other related languages. To do this, in addition to all that was attempted beside, would have extended the work both in content and in time of preparation, far beyond the limits assigned to it." A second edition, revised and extended, was published ten years later, in 1889. A 'Supplement to his Sanskrit Grammar: The Roots, Verb-forms, and Primary Derivatives of the Sanskrit Language,' 250 pp., was published in Leipzig in 1885. That he did not discredit and slight the old Hindu grammarians because of any lack of acquaintance with them is shown by his own work and publications in that field. He published not only the Atharva-Veda-Prātiçākhya (text, translation and notes, in 1862), but also a similar edition of the Tāittirīya-Prātiçākhya, with its commentary, the Tribhāshyaratna, in 1871. The true relations of Hindu Grammar to the study of Sanskrit, he made clear in two articles published in the American Journal of Philology, in vols. V and XIV. His last word on the subject was this: "I would by no means say anything to discourage the study of Pāṇini;

it is highly important and extremely interesting and might well absorb more of the labor of the present generation of scholars than is given to it. But I would have it followed in a different spirit and a different method. It should be completely abandoned as the means by which we are to learn Sanskrit. For what the literature contains, the literature itself suffices; we can understand it and present it vastly better than Pāṇini could. It is the residuum of peculiar material involved in his grammar that we shall value, and the attempt must be made to separate that from the rest of the mass." More than twenty-five years ago he called attention to the fact that the very title of Professor Goldstücker's paper 'On the Veda of the Hindus and the Veda of the "German School"' involved an evident *petitio principii*. The fair theme would have been 'The Veda of the Hindu Schools, and the Veda of the European School: which is the true Veda?'

The following extracts from a review by Hillebrandt in the fifth volume of *Bezzenberger's Beiträge* illustrate the reception generally accorded to the Sanskrit Grammar:—"Es handelte sich für ihn nicht um ein tieferes studium der einheimischen indischen grammatik, auf deren reiche beobachtungen unsere bisherigen sanskritgrammatiken fast ausschliesslich sich stützen, sondern um die erforschung des sprachzustandes, wie ihn die litteratur selbst aufweist.... Whitney's eigentliche aufgabe war es, in die sanskritgrammatik die grundsätze der linguistik durchgreifender, als bisher geschehen war, einzuführen und die sprache als eine historisch gewordene zu betrachten. Dies princip hatte eine beständige rücksichtsnahme auf den vedadialekt zur voraussetzung und verlieh Whitney's buche vorzüge, welche allein genügen würden, ihm eine hervorragende stellung unter den vorhandenen lehrbüchern anzuweisen. Die reiche fülle neuen materials, welches er ... aus allen teilen der vedischen litteratur herbeizog und in instructiver weise dazu verwandte, über das allmähliche aufleben und absterben dieses oder jenes sprachgebrauchs aufschluss zu geben, die durch reiche beispiele und aufstellung ganzer paradigmen illustrirte unterscheidung vedischer und klassischer flexion, die von der indischen grammatik vernachlässigte statistische beobachtung des formenschatzes in älterer und jüngerer litteratur—dies sind eigenschaften die es in dieser ausdehnung mit keinem teilt."

The Grammar provided an instrument which all Sanskrit scholars are now thankfully using.

Of the Supplement to the Grammar, von Bradke wrote in the third volume of the Literaturblatt für orientalische Philologie: "So anspruchslos das Werk auftritt, in dieser Weise konnte es nur von einem unserer ersten Kenner der altindischen Literatursprache, und auch von einem solchen nicht ohne lange und mühevolle Arbeit geschaffen werden."

In this connection we should be again reminded that Professor Whitney was one of the chief four collaborators who furnished material for the great Sanskrit dictionary published at the expense of the Russian government.

In March, 1864, Mr. Whitney delivered at the Smithsonian Institution a series of six lectures on the Principles of Linguistic Science—probably lectures which he had given to the Sheffield Scientific School the preceding year. This course was repeated before the Lowell Institute and published in 1867, under the title of 'Language and the Study of Language,' 489 pages. This was translated into German by Jolly and into Netherlandish by Vinckers. The clearness and conciseness of the statements and the soundness of the views, in a field where the wildest vagaries had prevailed, and where the imagination was still allowed rather free play, were recognized on every hand. From the time of the preparation of those lectures, Mr. Whitney seems to have devoted to this subject more attention than he had given before. In 1875 he published in the International Scientific Series a similar book, in somewhat more compendious form, on the 'Life and Growth of Language: an outline of linguistic science,' 326 pages. This was translated into German, French, Italian, Netherlandish, and Swedish. This last book grew out of his lectures to academic senior classes.

No one has done so much as Mr. Whitney to teach sound views of linguistic science. Although the writer of this sketch has not ventured to include a detailed discussion of his views, perhaps mention may be made fitly of two points in which he was in advance of his contemporaries: he was among the very first to call attention to *analogy* as a force in the growth of language, and the first (after Latham in 1851) to doubt the then generally accepted view that Asia was the original home of the Indo-Europeans.

Papers which had been printed in the *North American Review* and other periodicals were collected and, with more or less revision, published in two volumes entitled 'Oriental and Linguistic Studies,' 1873-74, pp. 417 and 432. The first volume contained papers on the Veda, the Avesta, the science of language; the second, on the British in India, China and the Chinese, religion and mythology, orthography and phonology, Hindu astronomy. The author's regard for his earliest teacher in Sanskrit is marked by his dedication of the first of the two volumes to "Professor Edward Elbridge Salisbury, the pioneer and patron of Sanskrit studies in America." The second volume "is affectionately dedicated" to "Professors Rudolf Roth and Albrecht Weber, my early teachers and lifelong friends."

His long experience as a teacher of modern languages and as a student of linguistics aided to fit him pre-eminently for the preparation of grammars, readers, and vocabularies of French and German for schools and colleges, and his systematic habits of work enabled him to prepare these easily. This apparatus met the needs of the newly awakened interest in modern languages in this country, and has done much to further this interest. These books are said to be used more widely than any others of their kind in America. Some of them are published in two editions, full and abridged. His desire for a reasonable and truly philological study of the English language led him to prepare for use in schools 'Essentials of English Grammar' (1877, 260 pages), which has been adopted extensively by the public schools of the country and is declared, by one who knows, to have had great influence on the study of this subject.

Professor Whitney had assisted in the preparation of the Webster's dictionary of 1864, rewriting the definitions of many of the important words. This experience, his keen sense of proportion, his practical turn of mind, his precise and concise manner of statement, his wide and varied attainments,—all made him a peculiarly suitable person to be the editor-in-chief of the great Century Dictionary with which the people of this country will long associate his name. His unfortunate illness prevented him from revising the work so carefully as he doubtless would have done, had he been in vigorous health, and some have thought that he should be called supervising-editor rather than editor-in-chief. As the dictionary stands, he cannot be held responsible for details; but his influence upon the work was strong as well as salutary. Though he might not mark the proof for a dozen pages, he would score the next page in a manner which set a standard, and showed what he desired the revision of the rest to be, while the whole body of editors followed the general lines which he had drawn.

In the list of his writings which was drawn up by Professor Whitney in 1892, one hundred and forty-four items are enumerated; but numerous minor articles and book notices are not included, nor his contributions to the great Sanskrit, Webster, and Century dictionaries, nor his oversight of the German dictionary which goes by his name. He wrote articles for the New American Cyclopedia, Johnson's Cyclopedia, and the Encyclopaedia Britannica. He was a frequent contributor to the *Nation* and other periodicals. In view of the importance and extent of many of his publications, his diligence and intellectual fertility are extraordinary.

As a teacher of advanced students, Mr. Whitney was exacting. A two-hour course under him in Sanskrit called for a larger outlay of time and effort than a four-hour course under most other teachers. He required precise knowledge of others as well as of himself. He was never deceived by glittering generalities, nor satisfied with approximate accuracy when absolute accuracy was attainable. He was modest, however, and while he would not allow the violation of well-established principles, yet in the translation of difficult and uncertain passages he never insisted on the pupil's adoption of his view.

In controversy and criticism, Mr. Whitney struck hard; his sword was piercing, even to the sundering of joint and marrow. But he was fair; he never misrepresented his opponent. He never lost his temper and struck blindly. He saw so clearly the absurdities and difficulties of a false position that he felt bound to present it as it was, yet without any thought of giving personal offence. For example, no one would suppose that he expected to offend his friend and teacher, Weber, by the remark that the latter had "unwittingly put himself in the position of one attempting to prove on philological grounds that the precessional movement of the equinoxes is from west to east, instead of from east to west" (Oct. 1865); but the criticism is very similar to that (which was counted severe) on Müller (July, 1876), that "even the aid of Main and Hinds could not keep him, in his astronomical reasonings, from assuming that, to any given observer, the ecliptic is identical with his own horizon."

The only prolonged controversy in which Professor Whitney was ever engaged was that with Professor Max Müller. His early relations with Müller had been pleasant, and he had supported the latter's candidacy for his chair at Oxford in 1860. His first public mention (1867) of Müller's work on the translation of the Vedas was very complimentary; but when the first volume of the translation appeared, his review of it was exceedingly severe. In the fourteenth volume of his *Indische Studien*, under the heading 'Zur Klarstellung,' Weber gives an account of the conflict. According to him, the real source of the controversy was Mr. Whitney's spirited reply to Müller's criticisms on the Böhtlingk-Roth Dictionary. "Whitney hatte zwei Vorlesungen Müller's kritisch besprochen,—scharf, wie es Whitney's Art ist, aber ohne irgend welche persönliche Wendung, so wie sich Gelehrte, denen es um ihre Meinung Ernst ist, zu streiten pflegen." The occasion of the contest was the publication by Professor George Darwin, in the *Contemporary Review* of November, 1874, of a report of Mr. Whitney's views. "Müller nahm sich denn auch gar nicht die Zeit Whitney's Abhandlung selbst zu lesen, sondern trat gleich in dem folgenden Januar-Heft der Review mit einer nur auf die Auszüge Mr. Darwin's basirten Gegenschrift hervor." Some have wondered that Mr. Whitney should care to follow up the matter so long, and even in 1892 should publish a brochure of 79 pages on 'Max Müller and the Science of Language: a Criticism.' But the question with him rose far above personalities: the truth was at stake. His mind, accurate by both nature and training, shrank from allowing inaccurate statements and false principles to be floated by a charming style. Great Britain in this generation has had more than one scholar of note whose brilliant form of statement, ingenious theories, and varied attainments have sufficed to give them undue authority on subjects where they made some grievous errors. Mr. Whitney felt that the higher a scholar's position, the greater his authority, the more careful he should be in all matters. He was heartily vexed by attempts to overlook and avoid the real point at issue. His vigorous spirit may have felt a certain enjoyment in a conflict; as an intellectual athlete he could appreciate the beauty of a keen thrust or the weight of a heavy blow; but while he did not fear a conflict, in some cases he avoided a controversy, even when he had been misunderstood and misrepresented.

No sketch of Mr. Whitney's character would be complete which did not mention his musical tastes. Music was always a source of pleasure and recreation to him. He had a fine tenor voice; and when a young man he was an acceptable and admired leader of the choir of Jonathan Edwards's old church in Northampton. The story is told that his conversations with the Rev. Dr. George E. Day, which led to his study of Sanskrit, were more frequent and natural because of his weekly calls at the pastor's house for the list of hymns to be sung. He was an active member of the Mendelssohn Society of New Haven a score of years ago, and did much to rouse the community to take interest in oratorios and other choral music, writing for the newspapers appreciative accounts of the works to be performed. He was prominent in securing for New Haven concerts by the Boston Symphony Orchestra. One of the last occasions which brought him into a public gathering was a University Chamber Concert by the Kneisel Quartet. He was fond of singing hymns on Sunday evenings, and while he cherished some of the old tunes of his youth, he welcomed the introduction of the modern more ecclesiastical music. While singing the old hymns he was as fervent and orthodox as his Puritan ancestors.

Mr. Whitney was no recluse, nor a typical professor in manner. He attracted men to him and enjoyed being with them. He was not at all emotional, however, and cared little for general society. He gave a rather extreme view of himself in a letter written in 1869: "I am of a more than usually reserved and unsocial nature. I avoid society as much as I can, and am never quite comfortable in the company of any excepting those with whom I am most nearly bound. My besetting sin is burying myself in my books and papers, and too much overlooking all that is outside of them,— partly from natural tendencies, partly because I feel that in that way I shall on the whole do most good and give most pleasure to others." His bearing was perfectly simple and unpretentious—in short, that of a gentleman.

Like Aristotle's "magnanimous man," he gave little heed to praise or blame—not being elated or cast down by either. He loved learning for its own sake and not for its reward of fame. The words which he wrote with regard to his friend Professor James Hadley are strikingly true of himself: "No one was ever more free from the desire to shine among his fellows. His was a modesty entirely unfeigned, and free from every taint of a lower feeling.... He devoted himself so entirely to truth and virtue and duty, as he knew them, that there was left no room for any thought of self. He neither extolled himself nor gave way unduly to others." "He knew his power, but possessed it in the spirit of moderation and reserve." He was eminently guileless—though by no means a subject for imposition by others. He would have made an admirable lawyer or statesman, but he could not have been a politician. He saw truth clearly and abhorred anything like trickery or disingenuousness. He was also thoroughly sane. Sentimental enthusiasm never led him to denote as certain views which later were to be proved false. He had few scientific retractions to make in the course of forty-five years of publication. His statements on uncertain points were carefully guarded. Where doubt existed, he was apt to feel it; in fact he was called in Germany "der Skeptiker der Sprachwissenschaft." His sanity restrained him from various excesses. His opinions on the desirability of reform in the spelling of the English language were clear and clearly expressed, and he was the first chairman of the committee appointed by the Philological Association for the furtherance of this reform in our country, but he saw so distinctly the difficulties in the way of an abrupt change, at least for the present, that he wasted no time in a Quixotic crusade. He was invited by the Japanese government to prepare an opinion in regard to the adoption of English as the official language of Japan—but he was not carried away by any sentimental notions of English as a *Weltsprache*. His mind was like a diamond, and his style was eminently clear and forcible. He never strove to be eloquent, but always expressed his thoughts in the fewest and simplest words. His was the style of a teacher rather than that of a popular platform-lecturer, but was enlivened by a strong sense of humor and by keen wit.

Professor Whitney's services to science and learning were freely recognized, both at home and abroad. He received the degree of Ph.D., *honoris causa*, from the University of Breslau in 1865; that of LL. D. from Williams College in 1868, from the College of William and Mary in 1869, from Harvard in 1876, and from the University of Edinburgh in 1889; that of J.U.D. from St. Andrews University in Scotland in 1874; that of

L.H.D. from Columbia in 1887. He was a member of the National Academy of Sciences; an honorary member of the Oriental or Asiatic societies of Great Britain and Ireland, of Germany, of Bengal, of Japan, and of Peking; of the Literary Societies of Leyden, of Upsala, and of Helsingfors; fellow of the Royal Society of Edinburgh; member or correspondent of the Academies of Dublin, of Turin, of Rome (*Lincei*), of St. Petersburg, of Berlin, and of Denmark; also, correspondent of the Institute of France; and Foreign Knight of the Prussian order *pour le mérite* for Science and Arts, being elected May 31, 1881, to fill the vacancy made by the death of Thomas Carlyle.

In 1870 the Berlin Academy of Sciences voted him the first Bopp prize for his publication of the Tāittirīya-Prātiçākhya, as the chief contribution to Sanskrit philology during the preceding three years.

The following extracts from a brief article in the *Berliner Nationalzeitung*, from the pen of Professor Albrecht Weber, form an interesting companion-piece to the letter from the same scholar, dated in December, 1852, which was quoted in the early part of this sketch: "Der jüngst in Yalecollege verstorbene Professor William Dwight Whitney war einer der ersten Indianisten und Sprachforscher der Gegenwart. Seine Sanskritstudien absolvirte er bei uns in Deutschland, hier in Berlin bei Weber und in Tübingen bei Roth. Beide Gelehrte betrachten es als einen ihrer schönsten Ehrentitel, ihn zum Schüler gehabt zu haben. Gleich seine erste Arbeit in den *Indischen Studien* ... war ein Meisterwerk und zeigte alle die Eigenschaften, die seinen Arbeiten einen so hohen Werth verleihen sollten, Klarheit, Sorgsamkeit, und Akribie im kleinsten Detail.... Heimgekehrt nach Amerika, ward er der Begründer der dortigen, jetzt in reicher Blüthe stehenden Sanskrit-Philologie, die sich besonders durch die von ihm speziell betonte *statistische* Methode grosse Verdienste erworben hat, u. A. durch seine Schüler: Avery, Bloomfield, Hopkins, Lanman, Jackson, Oertel, Perry, Smyth, Snyder, trefflich vertreten wird.... Seine Uebersetzung eines der ältesten vorhandenen Lehrbücher der indischen Astronomie zeigte ihn als trefflichen Rechner und Astronom. Schärfe der Kritik, Klarheit der Darstellung, Genauigkeit der Arbeit sind allen seinen Werken als Stempel aufgedrückt. Sein reifstes Werk wohl ist seine 'Sanskrit-Grammatik,' ... die erste *historische* Darstellung derselben, gewissermassen ein *gründliches* Résumé aus dem grossen Petersburger Sanskrit-Wörterbuch von Böhtlingk und Roth. Seine Arbeiten erstreckten sich im Uebrigen auf die verschiedensten Gebiete der Sprachwissenschaft.... Deutschland verliert in ihm einen der wärmsten Freunde, die es in Amerika hatte, Amerika einen seiner besten Gelehrten, und die Wissenschaft im grossen und ganzen einen ihrer ersten Koryphäen."

On August 28, 1856, Professor Whitney married Elizabeth Wooster Baldwin, daughter of the Hon. Roger Sherman Baldwin, of New Haven (ex-Governor of Connecticut and U. S. Senator), great-granddaughter of Roger Sherman, and great-great-granddaughter of President Thomas Clap, of Yale. Six children, three sons and three daughters, were born to them; of whom one son (the Hon. Edward B. Whitney, Assistant Attorney-General of the U. S.) and the three daughters survive. The daughters assisted their father in some of his later publications in the field of modern languages, and have done literary work of their own.

Just after a hard summer's work, at the very beginning of the college year in the autumn of 1886, Professor Whitney was prostrated by a severe disorder of the heart. For a time he was forbidden by his physician to do more than a minimum of work. He was obliged to avoid fatigue and excitement, and was limited strictly in his physical exercise. Those who had seen him return invigorated and exhilarated from a ten-miles' walk in the country were deeply pained to watch his slow, measured gait. He surprised many by his graceful submission to restrictions which he must have felt most keenly, and his household was still the brightest and most cheerful in the city. The gentler side of his nature became more prominent than before. His face grew more and more beautiful, with his white hair and beard, and delicate fair complexion. Though not an old man, he became truly venerable in appearance, and his presence was a real benediction to all whom he met. He was obliged to abandon entirely his work with undergraduate classes, but continued his classes in Sanskrit, receiving the students in his study at his home. During most of the past year he had six of these exercises each week. He did not abandon his other scholarly work. During the early years of this period of weakness, the Century Dictionary was going through the press and received his care. Every year witnessed his publication of some scientific paper or papers. He aided in the plans for the World's Congress of Philology, last year. One of his intimate associates, Professor Lounsbury, has written of him: "To me, at least, words seem inadequate to describe the quiet heroism which gave serenity and calm to his latter days, and the unflinching resolution with which he met and discharged every duty of a life over which the possibility of sudden death was always casting its shadow."

After an illness of about two weeks, Mr. Whitney passed away from this life, during sleep, on the morning of Thursday, June 7, 1894.

In the death of William Dwight Whitney, this country has lost one of her most distinguished men, one who had been recognized throughout the world as one of the highest authorities in his department of learning, and who had been for forty years the leader of oriental and linguistic studies in America and the personal master of a majority of the American scholars in his department. Yale University has lost one of her most brilliant and able scholars, one of her wisest and most faithful teachers, whose influence always made for diligent and honest research and statement. His publications have had a lasting effect on scholarship. His personal influence will long endure. In the words of Professor Lanman, "for power of intellect, conjoined with purity of soul and absolute genuineness of character, we shall not soon look upon his like again."

Thomas Day Seymour.

[1] The writer desires to acknowledge his special obligations to Professor Salisbury for allowing him access to original documents, and to Dr. Hanns Oertel for calling his attention to publications which would otherwise have escaped his notice.

Note

Note

www.ingramcontent.com/pod-product-compliance
Lightning Source LLC
LaVergne TN
LVHW041445170726
843492LV00008B/2814